Original title:
Purpose Found in the Simple Things

Copyright © 2025 Creative Arts Management OÜ
All rights reserved.

Author: William Hawthorne
ISBN HARDBACK: 978-1-80566-267-9
ISBN PAPERBACK: 978-1-80566-562-5

Moments Wrapped in Warmth

In a mug of cocoa, warmth does dwell,
With marshmallows afloat, just sip and yell!
Laughter bubbles up like frothy cream,
Life's funny moments, oh sweet dream!

Fuzzy socks slide on polished floors,
Tiny puppies racing out of doors.
Chasing tail, what a silly plight,
Under the couch, they're out of sight!

Threads of a Forgotten Tapestry

A threadbare rug holds secrets tight,
Where crumbs of cookies twinkle bright.
Silly stains tell tales of yore,
Of spilled juice and kids galore!

The cat sits proud on its woven throne,
Guarding its patch like a king alone.
With every scratch, it claims the turf,
Marking its territory with a purr and smirk.

The Kaleidoscope of a Garden

In the garden blooms a funny sight,
Dancing daisies in morning light.
Bees buzz by with a little jig,
Sipping nectar, then doing a gig!

The veggies plot in rows so snug,
Carrots gossip and tomatoes shrug.
Who knew plants could laugh like this?
Nature's humor, nothing amiss!

Tales of a Broken Clock

Tick-tock's gone on a wild vacation,
Leaving behind a humorous sensation.
Hands point to four, but it's half past five,
In this crazy time, we just thrive!

Watch faces laugh at their static fate,
Seconds freeze, what a playful state!
Lost in time, we dance and play,
With no worries, just seize the day!

Morning Light on Dewdrops

In the dawn's embrace, the grass wears jewels,
Tiny sparkles dance, defying all rules.
A bee sips nectar, with a clumsy flair,
Tripping on petals, unaware of its air.

Sunbeams giggle, as shadows play hide,
A squirrel joins in, with acorn as guide.
The world wakes slowly, with laughter and sighs,
In this cheerful chaos, wonder's disguise.

Tea Leaves and Tiny Moments

In a cup of chaos, the leaves swirl around,
Creating a potion, strange flavors abound.
A spoonful of sugar, like a sprinkle of cheer,
And a dash of my thoughts, just to keep it clear.

With each little sip, I ponder my fate,
What's for breakfast? Oh, toast can't wait!
The kettle whistles a merry little song,
In the realm of the mundane, I can't go wrong.

The Harmony of Everyday Sounds

The clock ticks a tune, oh so sublime,
As the fridge hums softly, keeping time.
A cat and a dog, with their playful barks,
Making a ruckus, brightening the dark.

The kettle is boiling, it sings like a star,
And dishes are clanging, a clumsy guitar.
In these quirky symphonies, joy often hides,
Tickling the senses, where laughter abides.

Embracing the Ordinary

Amidst cluttered desks and mismatched socks,
Lies the beauty of life in twists and in knocks.
A forgotten sandwich, with a story to tell,
About yesterday's lunch and a spellbound spell.

The dust bunnies dance, with a grin on their face,
Throwing a party in their dusty old space.
Life's hiccups and giggles, in every small chore,
In the dance of the trivial, we find it's not a bore.

Harmony in Simple Rhythms

In the garden, weeds do dance,
Sunlight gives them quite a chance.
With a squash and tiny gnome,
Who knew veggies felt like home?

Birds are chirping, quite a show,
While squirrels plan their acorn throw.
A cat just naps, so very chill,
While dreamin' of that tuna thrill.

Laughter bubbles, tea is brewed,
With cupcakes that are way past rude.
Each crumb smiles, that's no debate,
Life's delight can't come too late!

So here we sit, with all our quirks,
Finding joy in silly works.
Let's all laugh and sing along,
In simple things we do belong.

Cherished Moments in a Jar

A jar of laughs sits on the shelf,
It's filled with quirky bits, no elf.
A sock that's lost, a crayon stub,
And notes that say, "You're quite the club!"

Grandma's cookies, lumpy treats,
Are served in mismatched, funny sweets.
Each bite's a giggle, crumbs abound,
As puppy steals a cookie 'round.

Time trips by with shoe-lace grace,
When squirrels join the human race.
They chatter loud, and dance with glee,
While we all join, quite sprightly, see?

So gather moments, toss them high,
In jars where silly memories lie.
Embrace the chuckles, let them flare,
For life's too short, just laugh and dare!

Shadows of a Tired Sun

The sun yawns wide, in golden bed,
It wiggles warm toes, while birds are fed.
Clouds pull the blanket, oh, what a sight,
   Even the sun needs a nap at night.

The shadows stretch like cats on the floor,
Chasing their tails, what an age-old chore.
A squirrel giggles, steals a bright treat,
   Life's little ha-has make it all sweet.

Raindrops on Windowpanes

Raindrops dance, a tap-tap show,
Each little bead puts on a glow.
They slide and slip, a playful race,
Even storms can wear a smiley face.

Puddles form, a mirror of fun,
Reflecting the world when the day is done.
Jump in the splashes, oh what a thrill,
Every drop a blessing, an act of goodwill.

The Melody of a Quiet Stream

The stream hums softly, a bubbly tune,
It tickles the rocks, under the moon.
Frogs join the chorus, in froggy style,
And fish throw in splashes, with a cheeky smile.

A breeze blows gently, a soft touch
It whispers sweet secrets, not too much.
Nature's own jingle, out in the green,
Where silence sings loud, and laughter is seen.

Silent Words in the Wind

The wind tells stories without a sound,
It tickles the trees, all around.
Leaves dance in circles, a zany spree,
Whispers of laughter float wild and free.

A feather drifts down, a delicate sign,
That jokes in the air, are truly divine.
Nature's humor, in every gust,
Windy tidbits that spark our trust.

A Cup of Tea and Reflection

Steaming mug in morning light,
My cat gives me a judging fright.
With every sip, I take a pause,
Is this the life? A worthy cause?

The tea leaves dance, they swirl and spin,
While outside, squirrels fight to win.
I chuckle at their frantic race,
Maybe there's joy in a slow pace.

Dandelion Dreams in the Meadow

Dandelions sprout, a yellow crew,
Waving hello with the early dew.
I blow the seeds, they scatter wide,
Like my hopes when I step outside.

The wind tickles grass, a ticklish thrill,
I chase my dreams with a clumsy skill.
A bee buzzes by, I dodge and dip,
Maybe that's life – a whimsical trip.

The Meaning in Mundane Rituals

Brushing teeth while singing a tune,
Suds and laughter, morning's cartoon.
Each cycle brings its simple cheer,
Who knew flossing could bring such gear?

Eggs dance in the skillet, a little jig,
I flip the pan, it's quite the gig!
That yolk breaks free, it's running wild,
Ah, breakfast joys, just like a child.

Hues of Dawn

Dawn breaks, the sun starts to yawn,
In the sky, colors lightly spawn.
Pink and orange in a playful swirl,
It tickles my senses, makes my heart whirl.

I sip my coffee, feeling fine,
While birds chirp in a perfect line.
With every beam that hits my cheek,
I laugh at how nature tries to speak.

Hues of Dawn, Hues of Hope

With dawn comes hope, a bright sunny cheer,
A cat in the window, my furry dear.
He stretches wide, with a mighty yawn,
In his mind, life's flaws are all but gone.

Bread toasts, the smell starts to rise,
I watch the world through sleepy eyes.
With every bite, I find a grin,
In little moments, where joy begins.

Whispers in the Morning Light

The toast pops up with a mighty cheer,
Butterflies in the kitchen, what a bizarre frontier.
Coffee's aroma dances like a tune,
While socks play hide and seek, as if immune.

Pancakes flip with a plop and a splat,
Syrup pools like a lake, as the kids grow fat.
The cat watches bemused, eyeing the mess,
Guess some mornings are just meant to stress!

The Comfort of Unrushed Moments

Sipping tea while the clock ticks slow,
A sloth's pace is speedy, wouldn't you know?
The newspaper opens to a page long torn,
Who knew old comics could be so worn?

As neighbors yell from yards all around,
Their gossip floats high, a sweet, silly sound.
In hammock bliss, I swing and sway,
Mumbling to myself, it's truly okay!

Pebbles in the Path of Joy

Stumbling down the path, each pebble a prank,
One trips my shoelace, I'm far from a tank.
Laughter bursts forth like a fountain in spring,
Who knew a walk could bring such a fling?

Kids are zooming by, on bikes built for speed,
While I'm cringing, stuck by a stubborn weed.
Nature's bouquet decorates my fall,
Life's little stumbles bring laughter for all!

Breathing with the Breeze

With every gust, my hair's a wild scene,
A tumbleweed buddy adorns the routine.
Leaves are spinning past, a whimsical race,
I'm part of the chaos, a smile on my face.

Squirrels chatter loud, as if they know me well,
Scavenging snacks from my pockets, I fell.
Nature's lullaby, with birds in the mix,
Finding joy in fluff and silly little tricks!

Sunlight Through the Trees

Sunlight giggles, tickling leaves,
Poking fun at bumblebees.
Dancing squirrels join the fun,
Chasing shadows, on the run.

Branches sway, a silly show,
Nature's stage, a vibrant glow.
The wind snickers, rustling spray,
As birds rehearse their comedy play.

Leaves wear crowns of dappled light,
Nature's jesters, pure delight.
With every beam, the laughter drips,
As sunlight takes its playful trips.

In this grove, the joy's profound,
In every twig, a joke is found.
Even roots chuckle underground,
In simple things, joy's all around.

A Stitch in Time

A needle pokes with cheeky grin,
Fabric giggles, let's begin.
Threads intertwine in a twisty dance,
Sewing laughter, not a chance.

The bobbin winks, a prankster too,
Looping knots in bright shades of blue.
Sewing frocks, not just for show,
A patchwork quilt of joy, you know.

Pin cushions welcome all the fun,
Each pin a joke, like a pun.
Mismatched socks in the attic sway,
Remind us life's a stitchy play.

In every stitch, a tale we find,
Every rip, hilarious and kind.
So let's mend and laugh along,
For in our flaws, we all belong.

The Softness of a Cloud's Whisper

Clouds lounge around in puffy heaps,
Giggling softly while the sun peeps.
Whispers swirl on breezy flights,
Tickling the trees, oh what sights!

A cloud takes a nap, starts to snore,
Raindrops cheer, 'Let's roll out more!'
Sunshine pokes them, 'Not so fast!'
Chasing dreams of shadows cast.

With each float, a humorous tale,
Sky's fluffy comedians, never pale.
Laziness has never looked so grand,
As they drift in a quilted band.

Silly shapes for our eyes to spy,
Bubblegum creatures floating by.
Find your joy in skies so wide,
For in their whispers, laughter hides.

Dust Motions in Sunbeams

Dancing dust in a golden ray,
Chasing sunlight, come what may.
Tiny flecks in a vibrant jig,
They waltz together, not too big.

The sun plays tag with every floor,
Lifting dirt like it's a chore.
No broom can catch their lively spree,
They twirl and twist, carefree and free.

In the corners, they form a team,
Plotting how to make dust gleam.
A silly party on the shelves,
Where every speck is its own elf.

So next time you sweep or clean,
Laugh along with the dust unseen.
For in their dances, we might find,
Simple joys twirling in our mind.

Embraces of Familiar Hearts

In the kitchen, pots go clank,
While cookies burn, we laugh at our prank.
Spilled flour makes a snowy scene,
We dance in chaos, like a wild routine.

The cat's on the counter, a furry thief,
Knocking down spices, causing grief.
But oh, the joy in this tiny mess,
Each laugh rings louder, life's sweet success.

Grocery shopping, a jovial race,
Where carts collide, and laughter takes place.
Finding pickles in the fruit aisle's twist,
It's the joy in blunders we cannot resist.

Sunset dinners from mismatched plates,
Each bite like a story, with chatting fates.
Here in the clatter, our hearts intertwine,
In the art of the simple, we twinkle and shine.

The Stories Hidden in Everyday Lives.

A sock on the dog, it's quite the sight,
Chasing its tail, it barks with delight.
The cat just watches, unimpressed and keen,
While I catch the giggle through the screen.

Breakfast spills, it's syrup galore,
Sticky fingers, who could ask for more?
We toast to the mornings, slightly askew,
With coffee that tastes like a shoe that flew.

The neighbor's lawn, a jungle earned,
His lawnmower louder than bridges burned.
We wave like contestants in a funny fight,
Amidst the blooms, we find pure delight.

Evenings spent on porch swings sway,
As fireflies twinkle, they lead the way.
It's laughter that lingers, side-splitting fun,
In these tiny tales, our lives come undone.

A Whisper in the Breeze

A bubble-blowing breeze floats by,
Twisting my hair, it tickles and sighs.
I chase it down, and it leads me on,
To where daisies laugh, and troubles are gone.

A sandwich flies from a picnic spread,
As birds take their chance, we all duck instead.
Laughter erupts as the blanket takes flight,
In this crazy dance, everything feels right.

In the park, a slide turns laughter to screams,
With kids and their cakes, we're living the dreams.
The splatter of ice cream on eager chins,
In these little moments, true joy begins.

The whispers of trees, like secrets they share,
And if I listen close, I know they care.
In gentle breezes, and giggles that tease,
Life's little wonders put my heart at ease.

The Dance of Dandelions

A dandelion puff, a crown for the day,
I prance through the grass in a whimsical way.
With each gust of wind, I spin and I twirl,
Letting go of worries, just watch them unfurl.

A clumsy bouquet, stems bent and askew,
I present it with flair, just for you.
But bees have their plans, they buzz all around,
In this tangled garden, laughter is found.

Miniature picnics on checkered old cloth,
With ants joining party, like they own the froth.
Sandwiches squished, our drinks a bit spilled,
It's these silly moments that can't be thrilled.

When sunset arrives with crayons in hand,
We color the sky, each hue tightly planned.
A dance of dandelions, we waltz with the breeze,
In these simple delights, our hearts feel at ease.

The Sweetness of Homemade Jam

In the kitchen, jars all aligned,
Strawberries dance, so sweetly combined.
Splatters of juice on the floor I see,
Who knew making jam would be such a spree?

With sugar and puns, we mix with delight,
A spoonful of laughter, it feels just right.
Pop goes the jar, with a comical clap,
Now all that's left is to clean up the map!

A toast to the toast, with sticky fingers,
As friends gather round, the joy just lingers.
Fruits on the table and giggles, oh my!
It's banana bread next – let's give it a try!

The joy of the jam, it spills and it flows,
With every sweet bite, happiness grows.
So grab a piece of bread and a charm,
For laughter and jam, they both do no harm.

The Rhythm of Falling Leaves

Leaves do a tango, they swirl and they spin,
A delightful charade as autumn does grin.
Crisp crunch beneath foot, a playful tease,
Who knew nature's dance could put me at ease?

Squirrels hold their auditions, all fluff and no grace,
I swear that one chases just to win the race.
With acorns as props, they leap through the park,
What's better than nature's own jest for a lark?

The wind joins the party, a mischievous breeze,
Sending leaves flying, just like confetti, whee!
I twirl with them too, like a carefree ghost,
In the foolishness, it's joy I can boast!

So here's to the leaves, the laughter they bring,
In their floaty ballet, I hear nature sing.
With each colorful pirouette, I find,
In the dance of the leaves, I'm blissfully blind.

Hummingbirds and Heartbeats

Hummingbirds buzzing like tiny machines,
Flitting 'round flowers, like nature's routines.
With a zap and a zoom, they just can't be caught,
Their mischief is endless, with nectar it's fraught!

I sit with my coffee, a witness to flair,
While they flit and they flutter without any care.
It's like they're in training for some crazy race,
Or just putting on shows for our giggly grace!

Who needs a circus when blooms bring such joy?
Each flap is a giggle, oh boy, oh boy!
I'm left with my heart doing loops in my chest,
These creatures of whimsy, they truly are blessed!

So let's raise a glass to their darting ballet,
With laughter and chirps, they brighten the day.
These little acrobats, in sunlight they gleam,
In their zany dance, I find my dream.

A Blanket of Wildflowers

A quilt of wildflowers sprawls out in the sun,
With petals like laughter, they're having such fun!
Daisies are gossiping, oh what a sight,
While butterflies swirl in a dance of pure light.

In the meadow I tumble, like a child in delight,
With bees doing ballet, everything's bright.
A dandelion sneezes, oh what a surprise,
As seeds take a flight under open blue skies!

A picnic unfolds, with snacks on the grass,
Ants march in chorus, oh how they amass!
Nature's own party, with snacks all around,
Where laughter and flowers in harmony sound.

So here's to the blooms, each quirky little thing,
In their vibrant embrace, joy takes to wing.
I challenge you now, to find some wide space,
And lose yourself in this sweet, silly place.

The Beauty of Untold Stories

Underneath the bed, dust bunnies hide,
They plot and they scheme, with nowhere to glide.
Each tale unwritten, each fluff has a voice,
In sock drawers they whisper, oh, what a choice!

The pot in the kitchen, an old friend of mine,
Grumbles and giggles, it loves to dine.
With spaghetti in hand, it sings as it boils,
A chef in disguise, surrounded by spoils.

The cat on the fence, with a sunbeam so bright,
Watches the world, 'It's perfect, all right!'
With a flick of her tail, she gestures with flair,
For life is a stage, and she's queen of the air!

So laugh at the tales that the mundane has spun,
In every small moment, there's joy to be won.
For simple is grand, with stories to weave,
Embrace the absurd, and you'll never believe!

Savoring Stillness

In the midst of the shave, the soap takes a leap,
It bubbles and giggles, 'Come join, take a peek!'
A whisk in the bowl, it dances in glee,
'Beat me harder!' it calls, 'And just let me be free!'

The clock on the wall is a chatterbox too,
Tick-tock in the quiet, it wants to woo.
Each second's a wink, each minute a laugh,
It implores the old couch to just take a nap.

Coffee in hand, the mug gives a sigh,
With warmth in its belly, it starts to fly high.
A swirl and a twirl, it winks in delight,
'Life's too short for rush, let's savor the night!'

So sit with those moments, let laughter unfold,
In stillness, we find silly tales yet untold.
Embrace every giggle, regret not the wait,
For in simple joys, we discover our fate!

In the Cradle of a Simple Petal

In the garden so lush, a petal finds grace,
It twirls in the breeze, a delicate space.
Watch as it whispers, 'Life's often a dance,'
'Even weeds have their day, if given a chance!'

A dandelion's puff dreams of soaring quite high,
As children blow wishes, it scatters the sky.
With each tiny fluff, let the giggles take flight,
For who knew such dreams could ignite pure delight?

The snail on the leaf, oh, what a slow crawl,
With swagger and style, he giggles through it all.
'Why rush after time? I've got nowhere to be!'
Every inch a parade, just look and you'll see!

So cherish the moments that seem rather small,
For petals and puffs hint at grander life's call.
In giggles and grins, magic starts to take root,
Savor the silence, let your heart dance, then hoot!

Chirps and Chimes of Dawn

A rooster yells out, with a squawk and a flap,
'Wake up, sleepyheads, let's unravel the map!'
The sun peeks for coffee, a sip with a grin,
While the worms in the ground start their morning spin!

In the treetop, a squirrel makes breakfast with flair,
Who knew acorns could garnish a meal with such care?
With a twist and a toss, he dazzles the day,
'Just let me enjoy, while I scurry away!'

Chirps fill the air, a feathered brigade,
With songs that bring smiles in a grand parade.
They whistle and trill, a chorus of cheer,
'Time to wake up, the party is here!'

So welcome the dawn, let the silliness reign,
In the quirks of each creature, find joy in the mundane.
For laughter is golden, with every fresh start,
In chirps and in chimes, we discover the art!

Moments Wrapped in Silence

In a room full of chatter, I sneak a quick nap,
Ignoring the stories, the tales, and the clap.
A snore breaks the silence; heads turn in dismay,
I'm the star of the moment, come what may!

A tickle in my ear, a cat on my face,
Who knew my slumber would lead to such grace?
Laughter erupts as I quietly snore,
Turns out, peaceful naps are never a bore!

Letters to the Sky at Twilight

With crayons and paper, I write to the stars,
Dear cosmic buddies, let's skip the cars!
Please send down a comet for a joyride tonight,
I promise to wave, it'll be quite a sight!

My friend says it's silly, but oh what a dream,
A letter to Saturn with an adorable theme.
They'll chuckle and giggle, I know they will see,
The fun in the simple, just chatting with me!

Echoes of Laughter in the Afternoon

In the midst of tall grass, we hide from the sun,
With grandmothers watching, our sneaky little fun.
A game of tag starts, but one trips and falls,
And the laughter that follows, oh, how it enthralls!

We sip on some lemonade, sticky and sweet,
The joy of a summer that can't be beat.
Every hiccup, each giggle, like music so grand,
Life's funny moments, the best in this land!

Finding Gold in the Garden Soil

With a trowel in hand, I dig through the dirt,
In search of the treasure, avoiding the hurt.
A worm wiggles past, wearing a smile,
Turns out, not all gems are found in a pile!

I discover a beet, not shiny but round,
It's not made of gold, but it's fun to be found.
With each tiny spade, I uncover delight,
In the dirt, life chuckles, and everything's bright!

Wanderlust of a Coffee Cup

Every morning, bold and hot,
I dream of places I am not.
With a splash and swish, I sail the sea,
Not just a drink, but a travel spree.

From mug to desk, I take my ride,
To lands where sleepy folks abide.
Oh, the tales I'd spill if I had lips,
Brewing adventures with every sip!

In airports made of porcelain chic,
I brew my plans with a frothy sneak.
From bean to brew, the world I crave,
In a sip of happiness, oh, so brave!

So here's to the cup that knows the score,
Spilling laughter, leaving us wanting more.
Every sip a giggle, a frothy fling,
Oh, the joy a coffee cup can bring!

The Magic of a Sunset

The sun dips low with a wink and tease,
Paints the sky with colors like a breeze.
Clouds blush pink and gold like jam,
What's this magic? A visual slam!

I watch the world turn from day to night,
City squirrels preparing for flight.
The sun, a jester, bows so grand,
While shadows dance upon the land.

'Time for bed!' the day seems to purr,
As crickets serenade with a soft murmur.
But wait—oh no, I forgot my snack,
Sunset's beauty—hold on, I'll be back!

So here's to the sunset, a giggly show,
A spectacle that sets our minds aglow.
Simple wonders that make us grin,
In every ending, let the laughter begin!

A Seedling's Silent Promise

Tiny sprout in soil so deep,
Whispers secrets while I sleep.
With a wiggle and a gleam it calls,
Enough of dirt, let's break down walls!

Little roots stretching out for a hug,
Reaching for light, it gives a tug.
A green ambition, oh so spry,
"Watch out world, I'm born to fly!"

With each tiny leaf, the laughter grows,
A brave green rebel, it quietly knows.
"Sunshine, sunshine!" it shouts with glee,
While raindrops tap-dance on the leafy spree.

So let's celebrate the sprout's big dream,
A reminder that life's a silly scheme.
From humble starts, big things arise,
Laughter blooming under sunny skies!

The Joy in a Squirrel's Leap

Up they go, those furry delights,
With a flair for hops and dizzy heights.
Chasing tails in a jolly race,
They bounce like they own the whole place!

With cheeks a-puffed full of hidden snacks,
They leap and twirl; no time for cracks.
A little acorn could be their prize,
Yet watch them play like it's no surprise!

Through branches high, they dance and spin,
What's their secret? A cheeky grin!
With each plunge and flip, the laughter flows,
Squirrelish antics—the show never slows!

So here's to the leaps that catch our hearts,
In every bounce, a whimsy imparts.
Life's a playground, so climb and cheer,
For the joy in the leap is always near!

A Walk Amongst the Wildflowers

In a field of blooms so bright,
I tripped over a bee in flight.
He buzzed at me, "Hey, what's the rush?"
While I lay on the ground in a hush.

The daisies danced, they're quite the performers,
While I tried to dodge those sneaky wormers.
I laughed at the ants in their tiny parade,
Planning their picnic; we all should get laid!

The poppies swayed like a giggly crew,
I offered them snacks, they said, "We don't chew!"
But a butterfly landed, quite rude and spry,
He stole all my chips, then waved goodbye!

A walk to lose stress, I'd just like to roam,
With creatures around, I feel right at home.
In wildflower fields, life's shenanigans play,
Who knew simple joys could brighten my day?

The Secret Life of Shadows

My shadow told me, "Let's have some fun!"
We danced in the sunlight, both on the run.
He stepped on my toes, with a grin so wide,
   I laughed and I said, "What a silly ride!"

We played hide and seek with the tall summer grass,
   He ducked behind fences, oh how he'd pass!
   But when the sun shrank, he got quite shy,
   He clung to my feet, as the night rolled by.

I asked, "Hey buddy, why don't you chat?"
He muttered, "I mumble—don't wear a hat!"
   Together we ventured, side by side,
   A pair of oddballs, oh how we'd glide!

In the glow of the moon, we shared silly jokes,
   Creating our laughs like well-timed pokes.
Shadows aren't just darkness; they're comedy gold,
   Making the mundane feel wonderfully bold!

Songbirds at the Windowpane

Outside my window, birds start to sing,
With each little chirp, they announce spring.
A sparrow dressed up like a debutante,
Twirled 'round the branch like he's in a font.

A robin complained, "I lost my red vest!"
While looking so dapper, he passed every test.
A thrush chirped back, with an eye-roll and sigh,
"Look in the bushes, don't be so shy!"

The starlings rehearsed their newest hit tune,
While I made some coffee, hoping to swoon.
They laughed at my mug, painted with cats,
And harmonized softly while dancing on mats.

I clapped at their show, feeling lucky and blessed,
To hear such a concert, I felt quite impressed.
With feathers and songs, what more could I crave?
In moments like these, I feel so brave!

Crumbs of Contentment

I found crumbs upon my old kitchen floor,
A treasure trail leading right to the door.
I followed them, thinking, "What could this mean?"
Turns out they're just from yesterday's cuisine!

A mouse with a swagger, all decked in cheese,
Squeaked, "Welcome, my friend, won't you come and tease?"
I chuckled and said, "Your style's quite neat!"
He winked and he scurried, oh what a treat!

We shared little stories, he offered me crumbs,
I told him about life; he showed me the drums.
Together we laughed at the woes of our fate,
Mice have their secrets, and so do our plates!

So here's to the morsels, the bits from our past,
A reminder that joy doesn't fade—it can last.
In crumbs and in laughter, let's rise and be free,
Finding bliss in the simplest bits of debris!

The Sound of a Loved One's Laughter

In the kitchen, spills occur,
Giggles rise like a frothy blur.
Crumbs dance like they're on parade,
Joy is the mess that we have laid.

Tickles shared over burnt toast,
Laughter leaves behind a ghost.
Even when the eggs explode,
Glee, it seems, is quite the mode.

Slightly singed and slightly sweet,
Life's surprises can't be beat.
When a chuckle is the best dish,
It serves up every smiling wish.

So let the humor take the reins,
In these moments, love remains.
Each laugh a thread that weaves the day,
Coloring life in a warm ballet.

Paints of a Sunrise

The sky awakes in orange hue,
Like toast that's just been buttered too.
Clouds drip paint with careless flair,
Mornings dance without a care.

Sipping coffee, a sleepy sigh,
Birds gossip, oh me, oh my!
As sunlight spills from sleepy seams,
It brushes dreams in daylight beams.

Laughs among the coffee stains,
Sun-kissed banter, bright refrains.
Together, no need for a plan,
Life's a mishap, and we're its fans.

With colors spilling, joy ignites,
Creating art in our delight.
Each sunrise brings a silly grin,
As we revel in the light, within.

Notes Carried on a Whispering Wind

A breeze hums tunes from yesterday,
Whispers give worries a fun toupee.
Leaves giggle, shaking off their dew,
Every rustle a secret or two.

Gusts overhead dance with delight,
Carrying tales from morning to night.
As the branches sway and bend,
They conspire as kids on the mend.

Voices travel on soft-spoken air,
Tickling cheeks, no time for despair.
Laughter rides where the wind will lead,
Sprinkling joy in every heed.

With every gust, the heart takes flight,
Finding humor in every slight.
Nature's giggles fill the vast skies,
Oracle of fun, where freedom lies.

Time's Gift in a Meandering Stream

A brook gurgles, lost in thought,
Chasing pebbles, tangled in naught.
It swerves and bends, a playful tease,
Dancing around the ancient trees.

With splashes, it breaks all ideals,
Each ripple carries whimsical deals.
Time winks with a gentle plume,
While frogs croak in a sunlit room.

Rocks sit like grumpy old men,
While minnows dart and laugh again.
With glee, the stream slips through the years,
Echoing joys and silly fears.

Racing on, it knows no haste,
In its flow, no moment's waste.
With bubbles bursting into song,
Time's humor carries us along.

Quietude of the Ordinary

In a world where socks go stray,
The dryer swallows, come what may.
But in each loss, a laugh does bloom,
A single sock brings joy to gloom.

Coffee spills on crisp white shirts,
Turns a Monday into quirky spurts.
With each patch and every drip,
Life's silliness is a cosmic trip.

The cat's confusion with the yarn,
We watch and giggle, oh how they fawn.
In their madness, we find delight,
Ordinary moments, make us light.

A Stitch in Time

My pants have grown an odd little tear,
Out comes the needle, but where's the flair?
With each stitch that dances in a loop,
I patch it up, a clumsy troop.

Thread fights back, it knots with a scream,
Every tug feels like a wild dream.
But I chuckle as I pull it tight,
Fashion faux pas? What a wondrous sight!

At times, crafting feels like a race,
Can I make this disaster embrace?
Yet every slip and every spew,
Turns ordinary into a vibrant hue.

A Thread of Life

The tangled cords beneath my desk,
Are like my thoughts, quite a grotesque.
But amidst the chaos lays a choice,
To laugh it off, let joy rejoice.

The coffee machine's a warzone, too,
Exploding grounds in a messy stew.
Yet through the spills and all the grind,
I cuddle warmth of the easy find.

Life's tangled threads twist and swirl,
In the mess, there's a silly whirl.
For in each strum of fate's own lyre,
Laughter's the spark to lift us higher.

Radiance in the Raindrops

Raindrops dance on my window pane,
As I sip tea, forgetting the rain.
Each splash, a giggle from the sky,
Nature's tickle, who needs to cry?

Umbrellas flip like acrobats bold,
Colors collide with tales untold.
Puddles beckon with a siren's call,
Who needs a plan when you can sprawl?

Rubber boots clump with glee and pride,
Splashing joy like a living tide.
In the storm, we find our zing,
Who knew chaos could waltz and sing?

The Beauty of a Blushing Sunset

The sun dips low, a shy delight,
Painting the sky with giggles of light.
Clouds blush like teenagers at a dance,
Even the stars give a knowing glance.

It's a show, where night takes a bow,
The moon chuckles at what's on now.
An orange swirl, it's pure delight,
Nature's laugh echoes through the night.

As daylight bids a cheeky goodbye,
I see the blush paint the twilight sky.
In every fade, a hint of cheer,
Life's simple joys, always near.

Lanterns in the Twilight

A candle flickers with a grin,
It knows the dance is about to begin.
The shadows twist like silly sprites,
As laughter leaps into the night.

The bugs practice their waltz of love,
While squirrels plot a heist up above.
The moon just chuckles, pale and shy,
Watching mischief wink from the sky.

In the corner, a cat takes a nap,
Dreaming of finding the world on a map.
While kids play tag 'neath the stars' soft glow,
Life's little moments steal the show.

So raise a toast to the night so bright,
With lanterns that laugh in the fading light.
For joy sometimes hides in the simplicities,
Like catching fireflies and giggling breezes.

The Color of a Child's Laugh

There's a giggle that paints the air,
Like splashes of colors beyond compare.
In mud puddles, they dive and they dip,
With joy spilling out on every slip.

A lemonade stand run by plush toys,
Squeezed from the laughter of sweet little boys.
With each sip, a grin spreads wide,
As they negotiate candy on the side.

The playground's a kingdom made of dreams,
Where the slides shimmer with sunlit beams.
Each climb up high, a royal decree,
As the laughter crowns a day carefree.

So here's to the sound, so pure and bright,
That colors our world with pure delight.
For in every chuckle, there's magic anew,
Creating a rainbow in bright shades of blue.

The Secret Life of Starlings

A flock of starlings, so wild and spry,
They gather for gossip in the evening sky.
With feathers that shimmer like borrowed jewels,
They play tag and tease—those skyward fools.

They take flight to share their funny tales,
Of dodging the cat with its pointy nails.
With flaps and caws, they plot their schemes,
While cool breezes lift their fanciful dreams.

In the dusk, they form a swirling mass,
Like dance partners gliding—what a class!
The world looks up, their laughter commands,
While humans below just clap their hands.

So let the starlings be our guides,
In the symphony of life where joy abides.
For in their antics, we find a rhyme,
That laughter is timeless, dancing through time.

Echoes of Forgotten Lullabies

In the quiet of night, soft songs emerge,
A lullaby floats, a gentle surge.
With teddy bears nodding, in rhythmic delight,
While dreams swirl around like stars taking flight.

They murmur of cats and little lost socks,
Of bedtime snacks and old wooden clocks.
Each note tickles the air like a breeze,
Making bedtime battles feel like a tease.

The stars wink knowingly, all across the way,
As crickets chirp in a harmonious sway.
While drowsy eyelids flutter and close,
To whispers of adventures that night bestows.

With echoes of laughter, soft as a sigh,
These bedtime tunes float up to the sky.
For in the stillness, we find the fun,
In forgotten songs that brighten the run.

Sunlight Streaming Through Leaves

Sunlight dapples through the green,
Animals scurry, quite unseen.
A squirrel plots with all its flair,
While I sip tea, without a care.

The breeze whispers secrets loud,
To the trees, and they feel proud.
A leaf drops down, like a clumsy fool,
I laugh at nature's own great school.

Bees zoom in, wearing their suits,
Pollinating, with no disputes.
I toss my crumbs, a feathered show,
As a flock of birds starts to grow.

With every shift and every sway,
Nature's quirks steal the day.
In the simplest scene lies a twist,
That sparks a chuckle, I can't resist.

The Dance of Dust in the Afternoon

Sunlight beams, the dust takes flight,
In lazy spirals, a comical sight.
They twirl and glide, in a wacky race,
A ballroom dance in their tiny space.

Mop and broom sit, plotting their scheme,
As dust devils break into a dream.
Caught in chaos, they spin and twine,
A domestic dance, oh so divine!

In every corner where mischief plays,
Smiling dust bunnies join in the fray.
Each flicker is joy, a soft, silly cheer,
As sunlight reveals what's hiding here.

Even the clock seems to giggle away,
Ticking and tocking in its own way.
A minute spent laughing, no toil lost,
In the simplest joys, we find the cost.

Little Prayers in Gentle Waves

Waves roll in, a rhythmic rhyme,
Little shells whisper, 'We've got time!'
A crab scuttles by with a cheeky grin,
As I dip my toes, letting joy in.

The sea frolics, in sunlit glee,
Sending bubbles, oh-so-free.
A seagull squawks, 'Life's a breeze!'
While I watch, begging tides to tease.

Sandy castles rise, then wash away,
Yet kids keep building, without delay.
Each wave a message, a silly prayer,
As laughter mingles in salty air.

In this dance of water and sand,
Life's huge simplicity is perfectly planned.
With each receding wave, I find a gift,
In nature's laughter, my spirits lift.

Glances Shared Over Breakfast

Buttery toast, a crumbly delight,
Over coffee, we chat, laughter in sight.
A dog sniffs around, hoping for scraps,
While we munch on joy, filling the gaps.

Eggs sizzle, the pan starts to hum,
A breakfast chorus, oh, such fun!
Each bite a giggle, a fork's playful dance,
In our morning feast, we take a chance.

Syrup drips down, a sticky foe,
Race the pancake, who'll eat slow?
We fail with laughter, syrup galore,
In these little moments, we're never bored.

The day ahead waits, but who cares right now?
In breakfast's embrace, we make our vow.
To cherish the simple, the joy it brings,
As we share in glances and silly things.

The Glow of a Firefly's Flight

A firefly zips, all aglow,
Dancing around with a flashy show.
"Where's the party?" it seems to ask,
While we chuckle, it's quite the task.

In jars we dream up its grand parade,
But flickering lights—it won't be swayed!
It flicks and flits just out of reach,
Oh, the lessons that bugs can teach!

Caught in a net of our own delight,
We chase it down into the night.
But who knew the fun was in the chase?
Not in the jar, but in empty space!

So let it glow and let it fly,
We'll laugh as we watch it zoom by.
In the end, it's not about the goal,
But the laughter that tickles your soul.

The Weight of a Softened Stone

A pebble smooth and oh so round,
Sitting quietly there on the ground.
"Pick me up!" it seems to say,
But who knew it had so much to weigh?

I toss it high, and it rolls away,
With every bounce, it loves to play.
"Oh dear, I'm getting heavy!" it sighs,
As I laugh watching it dodge the skies.

A whisper of wisdom from a tiny bit,
In every rock, a tale is fit.
Though I'm weighing dreams on my own scale,
It beams back with a chuckling hail.

So let the smooth stone have its say,
Giggles are lighter, come what may.
In each little toss, we find the thrill,
Laughter makes even pebbles stand still.

Laughter in the Kitchen

The sound of pots with a clanging cheer,
A spatula spins while we all draw near.
"Oops!" is shouted with flour in the air,
While giggles bounce while we stir our fare.

The cookies burn but we just can't stop,
As we turn the heat down and the giggles pop.
"Let's blame the oven!" we exclaim with glee,
As we spoon out the frosting, oh dear me!

Chopsticks fly as we juggle with grace,
How did that carrot end up on your face?
But seriously, I can't take the blame,
When all that's left are our smiles to flame.

In chaos we find the sweetest delight,
Laughter echoing, such pure delight.
No recipe needed; just bring along,
A dash of giggles, and you can't go wrong.

Hidden Smiles of an Empty Chair

An empty chair sat still and wide,
With a blanket draped and dreams inside.
"Who will sit here?" it chomps at the bit,
As memories linger and laughter sits.

It's seen two kids playing peek-a-boo,
And late-night chats with the moon's soft hue.
Though nobody's there, it still feels bright,
Whispering secrets in the still of night.

A ghost of giggles tucked in the seams,
In the quiet, it bursts with daydreams.
"Come on, let's party!" it seems to declare,
As I plop down, with room to spare!

So here's to the chair, both sturdy and true,
In every absence, it's still got the view.
With smiles hidden and laughs so near,
An empty chair can hold so much cheer.

The Heartbeat of a Gentle Rain

Puddles form like tiny lakes,
Splashing shoes with joyous shakes.
Umbrellas dance like silly hats,
While raindrops sing to jumping cats.

Clouds are just fluff, we ride the storm,
In our raincoats, we feel so warm.
Every drip is a giggling sound,
Nature's jokes simply abound.

Not a worry for the wet parade,
We find the fun in every shade.
With each splash, a laugh we share,
Chasing rainbows through the air.

So let the skies drench us through,
We'll wear our joy like a rainshoe.
In every drop, a wiggle waits,
Laughter flows as nature relates.

Cracks in the Pavement

Sidewalks whisper, tales to tell,
Of how they fell, and then they swell.
Where grass pokes through, a rebel sprout,
Nature giggles, and so we shout.

We step on cracks, avoid the broom,
Superstitions dance in the gloom.
Yet every cleft has charm and glee,
A pathway to whimsy, can't you see?

Skaters slip, they find their thrill,
Dodging edges with flair and skill.
In every flaw, a joke resides,
A laugh shared wide with friends beside.

So next time you stroll in the sun,
Notice the cracks, add to the fun.
For life's odd twists can make us grin,
In little flaws, our joy begins.

The Depth of a Gentle Smile

A smile is more than lips that bend,
It's silly secrets shared with friends.
Brightening days with goofy grins,
Mischief starts where laughter begins.

With a wink, like a sneaky thief,
It steals away our little grief.
Every beam, a spark to ignite,
A beacon of joy when times are tight.

It dances in the corners wide,
Cheeses up those who feel like hide.
In a blink, it flips the frown,
Turning life's circus upside down.

Collect this treasure, hold it near,
For every smile shakes off a fear.
With goofy faces, we swap our style,
Unleashing wonders with a single smile.

Stones That Tell Tales

Oh stones, you've seen the ages turn,
From dino tales to fires that burn.
You sit so proud, like grumpy old men,
With stories etched that start again.

Skip me a stone and watch it plop,
Into the lake, it makes a stop.
Then with a splash, it sends a shout,
A ripple's giggle that spins about.

Each rock a gossip, each pebble a plot,
Whispers of history, no matter how hot.
With every toss, more yarns unfold,
In raucous rounds, their secrets told.

So treasure those stones that hold their ground,
For in their silence, fun can be found.
Nature's storytellers, bold and clear,
Adding laughter as they persevere.

Chasing Shadows at Dusk

A shadow flits across the ground,
My feet trip over, I turn around.
Caught in a dance with the evening light,
I laugh as I stumble, oh what a sight!

The trees stretch long like silly tall men,
Tickling the clouds with their leafy pens.
I chase after shadows, my giggles a spree,
What a ridiculous game, just the moon and me!

With each playful leap, I seem to confuse,
The night laughs with me, what a joyous ruse!
Falling on grass, my worries now fade,
Even my shadow is now mislaid!

So here's to the dusk, where antics reign free,
Chasing shadows is where I want to be.
Forget all the worries, just listen and hear,
The simple delight, in laughter and cheer!

The Pulse of Everyday Life

A toaster pops like a fireworks show,
While I dance around in my bunny slippers so.
Cereal bounces in a milk-filled bath,
Every spoonful giggles, sharing its math!

The sun's a lazy sloth, just peeking through,
I wave at the coffee, my morning brew.
It splashes back joy, in a mug it beams,
Who knew such small things could fuel my dreams?

The cat takes a leap, like a jumping bean,
Swatting at dust motes, all shiny and keen.
Each moment we share is a comic delight,
In the chaos of living, we hold on tight!

So here's to the laughter found in the hum,
Of life's little quirks, they make us feel young.
With whispers of joy in the mundane's embrace,
Every tick of the clock becomes a dance space!

The Weight of a Simple Stone

I found a nice pebble, oh what a thrill,
It weighs like my worries, isn't that a skill?
I tossed it in water, made ripples that swirl,
Watch it create giggles as the waves twirl!

In my pocket it rests, a little friend true,
A treasure of laughter, just waiting to cue.
I name it Sir Rock, such a dignified chap,
Together we plot mischief while taking a nap!

I dropped it on purpose, just to hear it land,
"Plop!" it exclaimed, as it grinned up at hand.
Not just a stone, it's a jester in disguise,
Laughing at life, in its carefree lies.

So here's to the weight of the stones that we find,
A bit of a chuckle, in our heart and mind.
For in every small thing, a big smile we glean,
The simple reminders where joy can be seen!

The Embrace of a Loved One

Arms that wrap tight like a burrito hug,
A cozy reminder, life's warm and snug.
In a moment we giggle, though tight it may feel,
Spinning in circles, it's a love that's surreal!

With every embrace, it's a dance of pure bliss,
Who knew a squeeze could feel like this?
We roll on the floor, in a laughter fest,
These playful embraces, they're always the best!

A tickle, a poke, and we both lose our breath,
Love's silly antics, it dances with death.
In the chaos of life, it feels just so right,
To hold onto laughter, with all of our might!

So here's to the hugs, where giggles collide,
In bonds that make living a joyful ride.
The moments may slip, but love is our tune,
In the warmth of each other, we're over the moon!

Notes from a Silent Observer

Watching ants march in line,
They're off on their lunch break, so divine.
Sipping tea on my rickety chair,
I salute their mission with flair.

A bird lands and fluffs its fine coat,
Chirping secrets, oh the gossip it wrote!
While I jot down these quirky notes,
With all my dreams afloat like little boats.

A cat prances by, such a grand show,
Chasing shadows of sunshine, oh how they flow.
Each simple twist of nature's play,
Turns my boredom to bliss, come what may.

In this stillness, life's dance is a thrill,
Every moment alive, with laughter to fill.
So I sit and smile, take it all in,
As the world spins around, let fun begin!

The Joy of a Quiet Moment

Sipping cocoa while snowflakes dance,
Outside the warm cabin, a prancing romance.
The creaky floor whispers stories so sweet,
Of socks mismatched and clumsy feet.

In the corner, a cat stretches wide,
Dreaming of birds on a lazy ride.
While I chuckle at memories, so bright,
Of hot chocolate wars that sparked such delight.

Outside the window, sleds whiz and glide,
While I chuckle and sip, they take a wild ride.
Oh, how I envy that snowflake thrill,
But in my cozy nest, I feel time slow still.

With every comforting sip I take,
I ponder the joy of a simple break.
And find that laughter comes soft as night,
In quiet moments, everything feels right.

Clouds Drifting in Daydreams

Lying back on a soft grassy patch,
Watching clouds transform, oh what a catch!
A bunny here, a dragon there,
Just a little magic hanging in air.

The sun winks down, making shadows play,
As I ponder which shapes make my day.
A sushi roll? A giant shoe?
Maybe a hamster in a tutu too!

Here comes a cloud, looking quite wise,
I think it just rolled out of the sky's fries.
While I soak in this whimsical show,
Laughter bubbles, oh where did it flow?

Drifting dreams, oh sweet silly thoughts,
In fields of imagination, who knows what's sought?
Each fluffy masterpiece floats on by,
In this crazy mind, I'm free to fly.

The Allure of a Dusty Attic

Up the creaky stairs, I take a peek,
In the attic dark, where adventures sneak.
Old boxes stacked like a tower of dreams,
With knick-knacks that giggle and softly beam.

A hat that's too big, a jacket too small,
Echoes of laughter bounce off the wall.
A dusty old typewriter beguiles my heart,
With stories untold, waiting to start.

I trip over memories, they laugh and dance,
Finding old photos, another chance to prance.
With old toys giggling in corners unseen,
In this treasure trove, life's so serene.

Each quiet moment filled with delight,
As dust motes spin in the soft sunlight.
In this attic world, my heart takes flight,
In the charm of these trinkets, all feels right.

Footprints in the Sand

Tiny footprints in the sand,
Pointing nowhere, isn't that grand?
Seagulls cawing, a real loud cheer,
A beach day well spent, oh dear, oh dear!

Sandcastles built with a big old grin,
Just to watch the tide roll in.
Buckets and shovels scattered around,
Finding joy where waves abound.

Was that a crab or my silly shoe?
Dancing in circles, the ocean's pas de deux.
What's more fun than a driftwood throne?
No one's the king when you're all alone!

So next time you're frazzled and stressed,
Remember the sand, it's simply the best.
A lazy day? Oh, that sounds keen—
Who knew living was such a routine?

A Journey with Paper Cranes

Folding paper, with skill or flair,
Crane by crane, without a care.
Each little flap brings giggles and cheer,
I think I've made five... oh wait, it's a deer!

Colorful flights through the air they soar,
Landing on my neighbor's porch door.
They'll wonder why there's a flock like a dream,
But do crabs take flight? Not on my team!

Origami skills? Oh, I'm a pro!
Just don't ask me where those swans go.
In the garden, amidst blooms so bright,
My paper crew's taken off for the night!

So here's to the cranes and their wily ways,
They dance in the wind and brighten my days.
Who knew simple things could really uplift?
Just don't forget to pack a snack... that's a gift!

The Comfort of Worn Pages

Old books stacked high with tales of yore,
Each page a comfort, like the shirt I wore.
They've got dust and dog ears, fun little snacks,
Who needs a theme park when you've got facts?

Worn pages whisper secrets, oh what fun!
Like old friends chatting, one by one.
Lost in the stories, oh, what a fling,
Reading 'til midnight, it feels like spring!

Sometimes I yell at the cover so tight,
'That's not how it ends, you're losing the fight!'
But books just chuckle, they're wise as can be,
Knowing it's all about you and me.

So raise a cup to every old tome,
They'll take you on journeys from your cozy dome.
Page by page, sniffing the glue,
I'll take a road trip, how 'bout you?

Stars Whispering Nostalgia

Under the stars, oh, what a glow,
Reminds me of marshmallows, singing, 'Hello!'
Twinkling like laughter, they wink in the night,
Was that a cow? No, just dreams in flight.

Shooting stars with wishes made in jest,
Like that time I wished for a pet with a vest!
But optic illusion leads me astray,
Now I'm chasing meteors instead of my way.

The cosmos laughs with a glittery grin,
Calling my name again and again.
I'll pack up my thoughts, let the night take wing,
Surrounded by starlight, I'm ready to sing!

So here's to the binding of moments we keep,
Memories bright, never too steep.
In the sky's embrace, I'm a curious sprite,
Dance with the stars, oh, what a sight!

The Embrace of Familiar Roads

On the bike, I ride with glee,
Pedals squeaking like a bee.
Sidewalk cracks, my trusty guide,
Pointing to where laughter hides.

Neighbors wave with coffee cups,
As I dodge the playful pups.
Every turn, a treasure found,
A world where joy is always crowned.

The ice cream truck, a cheerful sound,
Makes me dance and spin around.
With sprinkles on my tousled hair,
Life's sweet moments linger there.

So here I roam, a merry fool,
Chasing fun, that's my golden rule.
Through every street, my heart does soar,
In simple things, I've found much more.

Nature's Unassuming Gifts

A dandelion in my hand,
A wish awaits; it's boldly planned.
Blowing seeds, I share my dreams,
While ants march past in silly teams.

Raindrops tap a silly tune,
Calling forth the sun at noon.
Puddles splash with childish cheer,
As frogs hop by, "Hey, we're here!"

A crooked twig, my walking stick,
Proves nature's humor, quick and slick.
With every step, I laugh out loud,
In forests, I feel safe and proud.

Beneath bright skies, where shadows play,
I dance around on this fine day.
In every leaf, a story springs,
Life's little joy, oh, how it sings!

Reflections in a Puddle

A puddle forms, my mirror shines,
With dancing raindrops, life aligns.
I see a face, a silly grin,
And wonder where my fun begins.

With boots on tight, I leap and stomp,
Creating waves, a joyful romp.
A splash of mud upon my cheek,
In every droplet, laughter speaks.

Clouds above do twist and twirl,
I crack a joke; the skies unfurl!
Nature's laughter, bright and clear,
In every splash, I find my cheer.

So here I jump from side to side,
With puddles as my joyful guide.
In mirrored moments, joy runs free,
Reflecting all that life can be.

The Language of a Gentle Breeze

A breeze whispers through the trees,
Tickling leaves and buzzing bees.
It tells of secrets, oh so light,
Of silly plans for day and night.

With swinging swings and laughing parks,
The wind joins in with playful sparks.
A gust of fun, a friendly shove,
Reminds me of all things I love.

Cotton candy clouds float by,
While I chase dreams beneath the sky.
The gentle breeze, a constant friend,
In every turn, joy knows no end.

So let it swirl, let laughter rise,
As wind brings chuckles from the skies.
In every sigh-turned-giggle spree,
A simple dance, just you and me.

www.ingramcontent.com/pod-product-compliance
Lightning Source LLC
Chambersburg PA
CBHW051632160426
43209CB00004B/614